PORSCHE COOKS VEGAN

BY PORSCHE THOMAS

To

Russell Simmons

*my mentor, my best friend
and always
the fire under my ass*

TABLE OF CONTENTS

BREAKFAST

SOUPS AND SALADS

FAVES

HOLIDAY

DESSERT

EXTRA

FOREWORD

WHY

So you, the same person who for years maintained that you loved meat way too much to give it up, and that you needed more than just fruits and berries to live on, have decided to give this vegan thing a shot. You either read my friend Russell Simmons book The Happy Vegan explaining why the world would be a happier place if you became vegan or you watched any of the many films about vegan health (What the Health, Earthlings, Conspiracy or Earththings) like so many others and were scared straight and riled up. Regardless of the reason, now you, the person in the south who loves smothered chops; the one in the Midwest who swears by deep dish pizza; whoever showed up at Russell's compassionate Thanksgiving asking "Where the chitlins at". YOU have decided to give this vegan thing a shot.

Whatever your reason for doing it- you want to live longer; lose weight; compassion for animals; protecting our planet; you know eventually those chitlins are going to kill you; Beyoncé did it.... whatever it is, one thing is going to be true for all of you- You don't want it to feel like you are "giving up" anything. You don't want your meals to taste bland or to look unfamiliar.

You've used every excuse not to give up eating animals in the past, or to not even attempt it in the first place. Maybe you grew up with a tradition of eating lasagna every weekend, and can't imagine not doing that anymore. You think green juice is nasty. Collard Greens without ham hock or neck bones just isn't collard greens. Being vegan is too expensive. You love cheese way too much. It's too hard to find vegan options. Your palette just isn't suited for it.

This book is for you.

I decided to do this book because I want to help the doubters, naysayers and downright confused. The people I find at Whole Foods every week staring blankly at the vegan section with dead eyes. The amazing people who hop on my YouTube channel every time I post anything eager to grab on to any bit of information they can get theirs minds on. Anyone who's ever expressed to me in great detail the complexities of giving up cheese.

I always tell people that I became "kinda" vegan through necessity and "fully" vegan by harassment. Many years ago, I became very abruptly and violently lactose intolerant. I had been on a pinkberry bender, and then one day, after eating it (as I had been for about a week straight at that point) I got incredibly sick. My stomach cramped and churned. I began to violently throw up. Then I had to use the bathroom. It took the wind right out of me. It didn't get better right after. I was out of commission for several days thinking I caught some sort of bug. I drank loads of orange juice and brothy soups. I ate crackers and drank ginger ale. Once I began to feel better, about 4 days later, I made plans to go out. I attended an ice skating party and got hungry. I ordered the truffle mac and cheese, which I was excited about for obvious reasons. I started to eat it and it was AMAZING. But the closer I got to the bottom of the dish, the more I felt that feeling in my stomach again. Uh oh, I thought. I really didn't feel well. I just told myself that I came out of the house too soon, and that I was still sick, so I left the party and went home, stomach completely wrecked. I gave myself another day or two to recover before heading out again. While out, I ordered chicken fingers which came with ranch for dipping. I dipped the chicken into the ranch and barely finished that piece before getting that feeling in my stomach again. I got out of there like a bat outta hell thinking if I don't leave this second, I won't make it home and to my bathroom in time. I had to pull over several times on the way home, flinging my door open to throw up. That's when I made the connection, and then had it confirmed by my gastroenterologist. I was lactose intolerant. I was devastated. How would this happen like that? And all of a sudden?

For a while I was able to use lactaid pills to ease the symptoms and continue to eat my cheeses and pinkberry's, but it wasn't long before the pills didn't give me much relief anymore. That's when I started exploring recipes that were dairy free, and seeking out substitutions for the things that I love that I could no longer enjoy. That's when I had to get creative. During that time, I lived alone, so wasn't really buys and cooking any meat at home, and when this happened, I also phased out any dairy. So when I say that I became "kinda" vegan by accident, it's due to the fact I no longer kept any foods containing animal products in my home, and it really wasn't much of a choice for me. Yet, while dining out, I'd still indulge in very carnivorous activities.

Becoming "fully" vegan via harassment has a much simpler explanation. My best friend is one of the most famous vegans, Russell Simmons. And he harassed me about my animal consumption for years before all the knowledge he had been dropping over the years finally set in and I had my own light bulb moment. Once I made that decision and committed myself to making better food choices, I began to be more interested in the health benefits of going vegan. Sure, Russell had rambled on and on for years about them, it didn't really completely register for me until I started to educate myself about it. I ended up getting certified in Plant-Based Nutrition and learned so much. The more I learned, the more digging and researching I did. The more books I ready and documentaries I watched. There I was, several weeks before the due date of the birth of my twin boys, and I couldn't believe I had been putting into my pregnant body!

SO NOW, SOME VERY QUICK FACTS:

There's so much documented research proving that not only can you maintain a healthy weight and get most vital nutrients by following a plant-based diet, you can also prevent and even reverse many of the diseases that are the leading causes of death.

Eating animals is actually killing us, and we know this because we have 60 years of science as evidence. Thanks to the efforts of people like Colin T. Campbell, the leading biochemist most famously know for The China Study (the largest study of human diet ever conducted), we know that protein from animals promotes the growth of cancer cells, promotes obesity and diabetes, and promotes heart disease and high cholesterol, all of which are among the top 10 causes of death in the world today. There is also evidence that alludes to animal consumption, including dairy products, being associated with osteoporosis, Alzheimer's disease and many other diseases.

For people who are genetically predisposed to certain types of cancer, that in itself is not enough to make that cancer "active". However, what we know is that eating meat can "activate" that cancer, increasing the rate at which those cancer cells divide and multiply. That shouldn't be surprising since the World Health Organization (WHO) currently classifies processed meat as a carcinogen . On the other hand, switching to a plant-based diet can leave that cancer dormant, or even better, reverse progressive cancer by reversing the growth of the cancer cells. A vegan diet can also reverse diabetes, heart disease, osteoporosis, as well as lower your cholesterol and lower the current rates of obesity.

Something that may be considered less serious to some, but affects many more people, including me... lactose intolerance. Lactose, the sugar found in milk is not easily digested by humans after approximately the age of 5 years old, when we stop producing the lactase enzyme which breaks down that sugar. This means that over 60 % of adults are not able to digest milk and dairy, leading to many forms of lactose intolerance. Some people are even under the belief that going vegan causes lactose intolerance. Not realizing that being sick and feeling terrible had become the norm, and after going vegan and feeling better, "cheating" on their vegan diet with something dairy after finally feeling good makes the bodies reaction to dairy seem much more pronounced. In short, cutting out dairy will also just make you feel better, especially if you are someone that experiences the negative effects of consuming dairy.

I've only discussed the effects that eating meat has on our health. There are huge impacts on the environment as well, both on land and in our oceans. Going vegan reduces our water footprint by 60%, cuts planet-warming emissions substantially, and lowers energy and land use.

 Two thirds of all the agricultural land is used for grass and feed for livestock while only 8% is intended for the direct consumptions of humans. If we were to use the same land and feed to feed humans instead of feeding animals for human consumption, we'd have enough to solve world hunger.

Animal waste from factory farms have classified 55% of all US streams to be unsuitable for aquatic life due to excess nutrients. Additionally, the waste from farms move through local streams empty into the ocean into regions called dead zones and the excess nutrients cause the water to have little or no oxygen which kills aquatic life.

Trawling and longline, two of the most popular methods of fishing are also causing a lot of damage to our marine life and ocean ecosystem. Trawling, the act of scraping the ocean floor with a wide net affects a land mass that is 150 times worse than the damage that is being done to the rainforests. Not only does this have huge negative impacts, turning sea beds into deserts, it also affects many species of marine life due to the fact that 70% of what is caught are not the intended species and subsequently thrown back into the ocean as dead discard. Longline fishing, the act of casting lines up to 6 miles long with thousands of baited hooks, is responsible for killing hundreds of thousands of unintended species including seabirds, turtles, sharks, dolphins and whales. All of this leads to a major decline of species diversity in our oceans. It is estimated that by the year 2048, there will be no more seafood at the rate we're currently going.

HOW

I've watched my brother make the commitment to end poisoning his body. He read and read all about the bad things that comprised the food industry and all the ways it harmed the human body. He really educated himself on what not to put into his body and made the abrupt decision to eliminate as many of those toxins as he could. This sounds great, right? Not entirely. In the months after he stopped eating meat, and many of the other harmful foods that he'd read about, he'd lost almost thirty pounds. Not because he was led to some amazing diet, but because he found himself often staring into the refrigerator dumbfounded. While he did all his research to discover what not to put into his body, he failed at doing any to discover what he should be eating. He spent months hungry all the time!

If the goal in becoming Vegan is to lose weight, you need to do your homework in order to be able to sustain your weight loss. If your goal is to live a healthier lifestyle, you need to do your homework in order to sustain this new eating habit. If the goal is to be more compassionate, you need to do your homework, in order to keep things in the kitchen interesting, so you're not living solely on lentils and green juices. What I am getting at is that you need to do your homework!

In order to begin and maintain a healthy consistent vegan diet, I believe it may be more approachable by taking steps. First, you'd need to rid your home of non-vegan staples and replace them with vegan ones. Get rid of your milk, and get into some almond milk or coconut milk, or even rice milk. Toss out all your butter, and discover the wonderfulness that is Earth Balance. Lose the honey and check out a high-grade maple syrup or agave nectar. Replace any and all pastas made with egg with a brown-rice, quinoa or whole wheat pasta. These minor steps are a great way to begin to ease yourself into veganism.

If the goal is overall wellness, why not also chuck your rice and breads, and replace them with quinoa and sprouted bread. Forget about potatoes, and discover cauliflower, sweet potatoes and butternut squash.

To begin to change your eating and shopping habits, you'll need a nice base... things that you pretty much always have in your refrigerator and cabinets. So why don't we just start there:

Milk substitutes- Explore all of your options, and see which you like best, and what you like it best for. For example, for creamy smoothies, I love almond milk (I prefer unsweetened original flavored). If I'm going for a lighter tasting smoothie, I'd use a coconut milk instead (coconut water can be used for maximum "lightness." For stews and soups, I lean more toward canned coconut milk or even a richer coconut cream, unless it's a puree (cream of...), then I go right back to my basic almond milk.

Nutritional Yeast- Think about a time you've been in love, and you thought to yourself, "where have you been all my life!". This is how I feel about nutritional yeast. It's essential for most nut cheeses, and works lovely as a topping or garnish. I even like to use it as a Parmesan cheese substitute topped on mac and cheese or pasta dish. It's nutty flavor and flakey consistency makes it a very versatile companion to many types of dishes and snacks.

Cheese- Love cheese? So did I! Whether it be purchasing a cheese substitute or learning how to make specific nut cheeses, there are amazing options out there now. A favorite is Daiya©. The great thing about the Daiya© brand is that it is Dairy-Free, Soy-Free and Gluten-Free! Depending on your local grocer, you can find a variety of different flavors including cheddar, mozzarella and pepper jack, and come in the forms of shreds, blocks, slices, and cream cheese. I love Daiya© because it melts and stretches, meaning you can use it for anything from salads to sandwiches, pasta dishes to dips, homemade pizzas to homemade mac and cheese! Daiya© also offers a variety of yogurts, spreads and other wonderful vegan indulgences. If you're looking for a "fancy cheese" option, for say a cheese platter or just to snack on with crackers, try Miyoko's©. I really couldn't believe the way they nailed the consistency and taste of their 10 plus flavors, most of which are also soy-free!

Earth Balance- It's still butter-y! This creamy spread is so good, you don't actually feel like you're substituting. It's amazing on the simplest toast, and great for your most complicated baking recipe. It also doesn't contain any trans-fat or GMO's and it's gluten free! If you want opt for something sans Palm Oil, Trader's Joe's recently began selling Miyoko's Vegan Butter!! If you can't find a Trader Joe's near you, also try your local Whole Food's or order it directly from miyokoskitchen.com

Protein- When eating a vegan diet, it's important to make sure your body is getting the necessary amount of protein for you to thrive. To help with this, it's very useful to always have a hefty supply of beans and legumes, nuts, veggies, quinoa and other foods high in protein stocked. It's pretty easy to throw together a quick dish, or easy snack using these, making it not only very beneficial to your health, but also making your life just a little bit easier.

Avocado- This "good fat" can be used a multitude of ways. It can be used as a thickening agent for smoothies, a spread for morning toast, a creamy base for vegan chocolate or just as a snack- halved, salted, and enjoyed with a spoon.

You should know, going vegan will change your palette. You may have tried a friend's green juice ages ago and thought it was completely disgusting and tasted like grass. Guess what? So did pretty much everyone. If you're used to drinking sweet juices and sodas, then anything without high fructose corn syrup will probably taste funny to you. However, this is temporary. Processed foods are so heavily seasoned with salt, fat and sugar that they've dulled your taste buds over time. So things that are more natural may seem to have no taste or even have a taste that you may not like. The good news is, the human body is so capable of so many things. Your taste buds are adaptable. It can take only a couple of weeks of trying new things for your taste buds to actually re-awaken to the subtle flavors in many vegan delicacies. You can and will acquire new tastes, and not only can you learn to love the tastes of "healthy" foods... in doing so, your body can also learn to dislike the tastes of a lot of unhealthy ones. You can easily get to a place where your green juice will taste so much better than any soda.

Juices and smoothies tend to be a big part of a vegan's diet. It's a great way to start the day or satisfy an evening sweet craving. In smoothies, it's important to have a base (such as almond milk, coconut milk, coconut water, etc.) to allow the fruit and greens (if adding any) to liquefy. Adding a leafy green to your smoothie can increase its health benefits, and you won't even taste it (though it's more than likely to change the color of your beverage to green). Most smoothies will need either a banana or some avocado to create that thick "smoothie" consistency that makes it filling. Rolled oats can achieve this as well. In juices, it's important to include a watery veggie (cucumber, celery, etc.) to be able to add volume to your juice as well as dilute the strong taste of some other ingredients, such as beets or ginger for example.

Smoothies are great if you're someone who is on the go. If breakfast is not your thing, or you're a craver of late night sweets, or if you're looking to substitute meals with liquids, smoothies are a great go-to. First, it's pretty difficult to get the recommended amount of fiber just by eating fruit, so blending several fruits together to into a manageable glass to drink is a great way to get the necessary fiber. Not to mention, so many fruits have amazing benefits. Bananas strengthen bones. Blueberries are a super fruit said to combat cancer, protect your heart, promote digestion and stabilize blood sugar. Cherries are believed to slow the aging process as well as aid in insomnia and shield against Alzheimer's. Figs promote weight loss, lower cholesterol and controls blood pressure. Adding things like cinnamon, ginger, maple syrup and avocado not only enhance the flavor and/or consistency. These gems also have amazing benefits. Cinnamon can lower blood sugar levels and reduce heart disease risk factors. Ginger is great for anyone with stomach problems. Maple syrup contains high amounts of zinc, manganese, potassium and calcium. Avocados, also known as the good fat, contains omega-3 fatty acids (great for reducing risks for heart disease, high cholesterol and high blood pressure) as well as vitamin E and Vitamin C.

Superfood seeds are a great source for protein and an easy addition to any smoothie. I tend to just pick one based on what's available to me at any given time in my arsenal of healthy foods! Three of the most popular are Chia seeds, Flax Seeds, and Hemp Seeds. Chia is of the mint family, and is able to absorb up to 10 times its weight in water (resembling a tapioca, but without the sugar). For each three-tablespoon serving, you'll find 10g fiber and 5g protein. I love to prep chia seed pudding cups for an easy grab and go breakfast topped with fruit and granola. Hemp is a cannabis plant, but no, it's not meant to make you high! It's a protein that takes longer to digest, making you feel full longer. It also contains Vitamin E and zinc, which are great for the immune system. For each ounce, you can find 10g protein. Flax is the slightly nutty superfood seed that helps aid in digestion. It is thought to help lower blood pressure and cholesterol, and contains 8g fiber and 12g fatty acids per serving. It's also a good source of magnesium, which acts as an energy booster. Flax can be found either ground or in oil form.

Juicing: is a great start for the converting vegan as it helps promote healthy eating habits. Juices are another way to get your fibers, but mostly from vegetables as opposed to fruit. Like fruit, many vegetables have many amazing benefits. Beets control blood pressure, strengthens bones and aids in weight loss. Carrots saves eyesight, combats cancer, aids in digestion and protects your heart. Kale aids in blood clotting and promotes healthy vision. Spinach is an antioxidant which acts as an anti-inflammatory and strengthens the immune system as well as promotes healthy glowing skin.

Adding a fruit, such as an apple or a pear can take your juice from drab to delightful by adding just enough sweetener and plenty of additional health benefits. Adding cayenne pepper to your drink can help with an array of issues ranging from cold and flu to migraines and even digestion. It also acts as an anti-irritant and anti-allergen, and can promote detox support and weight-loss.

It's important to note... many of these health benefits are lost a few minutes after your juice is prepared, so it's really important to drink your juice immediately to obtain its maximum benefits. However, if you are unable to consume your juice immediately, you should pour it into an airtight jar or container within 20 minutes. Doing this will allow it to last up to 3 days in the fridge.

Soy: Soy is high in phytic acid, meaning that any foods you eat which contain soy will have less of its nutritional value. If you eat enough of those foods and also look to those foods as your main source for those nutrients, you can become deficient in said nutrients. Additionally, if you are eating soy that is a genetically modified organism (GMO), that means that you are consuming soy which has been affected to survive pesticide exposure making it carcinogenic (cancer causing). This is actually hard to avoid since about 91% of soybeans are genetically engineered.

There are an increasing number of soy-free options being rolled out regularly, which I find to be incredibly exciting. However, sometimes you will eat soy. That's ok. It's just important to keep in mind that unprocessed, ferments and organic soy are always going to be your best bet. When shopping look for Non-GMO and in the ingredients list, look for organic soybean and steer clear of soy protein isolates.

Gadgets: Going vegan has allowed the kitchen to become a total playground. There are so many toys that can help with your journey. You won't need to run out right away and spend hundreds or thousands of dollars on appliances, but there are a few things that can help make the transition a smoother one. First, you will need a good blender. For all of my nut cheese, smoothies, gravy's, soups and purees, a great blender is key. You can splurge and get a vitamix which works as a juicer as well, but that's absolutely not necessary. Another toy you may want to invest in is a food processor. It helps save a ton of time on chopping and mixing, and can be useful when making thicker batters. I also highly recommend investing in a great set of knives. It also saves on a ton of time, and makes prep overall much more enjoyable.

One of the biggest reasons I've heard for not going vegan is that "It's too expensive." I'm not going to pretend that being vegan is "cheap", but I will say that it is not necessarily more expensive than the way that you are currently eating. Let's face it, meat is expensive. On the flip side, supplements can be pricey as well. Consider the fact that while you are adding things to your diet and shopping list, you are also eliminating just as many things. There was a time when I would agree that the "vegan version" of many things was less in demand and therefore, more expensive. This is no longer necessarily true. There are now so many options and versions of vegan products, and the demand has become so much higher, that it's sort of caused the prices of many of these items to level out with their non-vegan counterparts. Another thing to consider is that by going vegan, you may find yourself preparing more of your meals, eliminating a lot of your "eating out" costs. Instead of buying your produce at the neighborhood supermarket, you may find yourself hitting up local farmers' markets (which I highly recommend) where you can certainly get better deals as well as way better quality.

For those living in communities where some healthy ingredients are harder to come by, there are now companies out there that will bring some many healthy ingredients right to your door for very comparable-to-store prices. One of those options is Thrive Market, an online membership shopping experience (think Costco, Sam's Club, BJ's) that allows you to have access to many of the products you may not have access to in your community with home delivery to the continental Unites States, giving so many the option to healthy foods. Having just become a mother and finding it hard to leave the house for certain necessities at times, I've finally really discovered the blessing that is Amazon! Oh em gee. Where have you been my whole life! There's Amazon Prime©, where for $99 a year, you can get free 2-day delivery on almost anything. So a lot of the supplements or dry ingredients that may be difficult to find in your neighborhood can be delivered right to your doorstep. Additionally, depending on where you are located, Amazon has begun rolling out Amazon Now©, which allows certain grocery items to be delivered to your door the very same day!

Taking on the challenge of becoming vegan will get you to start becoming more resourceful. `You will find yourself googling how to create vegan versions of your favorite dishes. You will discover an urge to discover more ways to improve your overall wellness whether it be from exercise, meditation, beauty regiments, etc.   This one change will improve your life. You will feel better. You will look better. You will want to share it with your loved ones, as this type of happiness is contagious.

You will learn to understand food, which will create a deeper appreciating for food, and why shouldn't we appreciate the things we are putting into our bodies? Why shouldn't we be in control of what we eat by eliminating the harmful ingredients that fill most of the processed foods that are made easily available to us and cause harm and suffering. The food and farming industries will not change until we force them to. Why not take control of your body, and take the power away from big business? This can be done, one recipe at a time!

SMOOTHIES

Blueberry Peanut-Butter Smoothie

Acai Berry Smoothie

Chocolate Date Smoothie

Pear Avocado Grape Smoothie

Pineapple Kale Smoothie

Strawberry, Banana and Coconut Smoothie

Green Pineapple Smoothie

Peach Oat Smoothie

Green Pineapple Smoothie

BLUEBERRY PEANUT-BUTTER SMOOTHIE

Serves 2

1 banana fresh or frozen

1-cup frozen blueberries

1 tbsp. peanut butter

1-cup non-dairy milk (almond milk, coconut milk, rice milk, soy milk)

1 tbsp. hemp seeds

Combine all ingredients into a blender. Blend until completely smooth, about

ACAI BERRY SMOOTHIE

Serves 2

2 packets (7 ounces) raw, frozen unsweetened acai pulp, lightly thawed

1 cup frozen blueberries

1 medium banana

1-cup coconut water

1 tbsp. agave nectar

Combine all ingredients into a blender. Blend until completely smooth, about
a minute. Enjoy!

CHOCOLATE DATE SMOOTHIE

Serves 2

2 cups almond milk

1 large banana

2 tbsp. raw cacao powder

1 tbsp. flax seeds

4 dates, pitted

1-cup crushed ice

Combine all ingredients into a blender. Blend until completely smooth, about a minute. Enjoy!

PEAR AVOCADO GRAPE SMOOTHIE

Serves 2

1 large pear

½ cup green grapes

¼ avocado

2 tsps. agave nectar

1 tsp. lemon juice

Combine all ingredients into a blender. Blend until completely smooth, about a minute. Enjoy!

PINEAPPLE KALE SMOOTHIE

Serves 2

1-cup pineapple

1 small orange, peeled

½ banana

4 large kale leaves (or big handful)

1 cup almond milk

½ cup coconut water

Combine all ingredients into a blender. Blend until completely smooth, about a minute. Enjoy!

STRAWBERRY BANANA AND COCONUT SMOOTHIE

Serves 2

6-8 strawberries, frozen or fresh

1 ½ cup mangoes, frozen or fresh

½ cup coconut milk

½ cup coconut water

Combine all ingredients into a blender. Blend until completely smooth, about a minute. Enjoy!

CHERRY SMOOTHIE

Serves 2

1 cup cherries, frozen or fresh

½ cup mango, frozen or fresh

1 cup almond/coconut milk

1 tbsp. coconut oil

Combine all ingredients into a blender. Blend until completely smooth, about a minute. Enjoy!

PEACH OAT SMOOTHIE

Serves 2

2 cups frozen peaches

12 tbsp. chia seeds

¼ cup rolled oats

1 small frozen banana

¼ fresh orange juice

½ cup unsweetened almond milk

1 tbsp. maple syrup

Combine all ingredients into a blender. Blend until completely smooth, about a minute. Enjoy!

CHERRY SMOOTHIE

GREEN PINEAPPLE SMOOTHIE

Serves 2

1-cup pineapple, fresh or frozen

½ frozen banana

½ coconut water

½ water

¼ cup fresh parsley

¼ avocado

1 tsp. freshly ground ginger

½ tsp. hemp seeds

Combine all ingredients into a blender. Blend until completely smooth, about a minute. Enjoy!

JUICES

Greens Tonic

Sweet Green Juice

Carrot Juice

Carrot and Orange Juice

Pineapple Cooler

Citrus Blast

Beet Juice

Sweet Potato Orange

Digestion Pleaser

Wellness Ginger Shot

SWEETGREEN JUICE

Serves 2

1 large cucumber, peeled

1 heaping handful kale

3 ribs celery

1 apple

½ cup mint

Add all items to juicer. Serve immediately

GREEN TONIC

Serves 2

1 cucumber, peeled

4 celery ribs

6-8 kale leaves

1 small handful parsley

½ lemon (rind removed)

1-inch ginger root (peeled)

Add all items to juicer. Serve immediately.

CARROT AND ORANGE JUICE

Serves 2

2 oranges, peeled

4 carrots, peeled

2 celery ribs

Add all items to juicer. Serve immediately.

CARROT JUICE

Serves 2

4 carrots, peeled

4 ribs celery

1 apple

1-inch ginger root, peeled

Add all items to juicer. Serve immediately.

CITRUS BLAST

Serves 2

Citrus Blast

3 oranges, peeled

1 grapefruit, peeled

1 lemon, peeled

Add all items to juicer. Serve immediately.

PINEAPPLE COOLER

Serves 2

¼ pineapple

2 cucumbers

3 celery stalks

1 lemon, peeled

Add all items to juicer. Serve immediately.

BEET JUICE

BEET JUICE

Serves 2

1 large beet, washed and cut into wedges

2 medium carrots

4 ribs celery

1-inch ginger root, peeled

1 medium apple

Add all items to juicer. Serve immediately.

DIGESTION PLEASER

Serves 2

¼ whole pineapple (or 1 cup)

1 yellow grapefruit

1 ruby grapefruit

1 lemon

2 stalks celery

1 carrot

Add all items to juicer. Serve immediately.

SWEET POTATO ORANGE

Serves 2

4 stalks celery

3 carrots

3 small sweet potatoes

2 oranges

1-inch ginger root, peeled

Add all items to juicer. Serve immediately.

WELLNESS GINGER SHOT

Serves 2

1-inch ginger root, peeled

½ lemon, peeled

⅛ tsp. cayenne pepper

Add all items to juicer. Top with cayenne pepper. Mix and serve immediately.

BREAKFAST

Breakfast Cereal

Sweet Breakfast Potatoes

Simple Avocado Toast

Acaí Bowl

Homemade Chia Seed Pudding Parfait

Stuffed Warm Apple

Cold Mornin' Oatmeal

Jamaican Style Plantain Porridge

SWEET BREAKFAST POTATOES

Serves 4

1½ lbs. sweet potatoes, washed, peeled and cut into ½ inch cubes

1 small onion, diced

½ red pepper, diced

½ green pepper, diced

salt and pepper to taste

Dash Thyme

Dash cayenne pepper

3 tbsp. olive oil

In a medium stockpot, cover the cubed sweet potato with water and bring to a boil. Cook only until tender, about 5 minutes. Drain. Set aside.

In the large skillet, heat olive oil over medium heat. Add onions, peppers and seasoning and brown. Once onions are caramelized, add potatoes and cook until browned.

BREAKFAST CEREAL

Serves 4

2 cups water

1-cup quinoa, rinsed

3 tbsp. brown sugar

⅛ tsp. cinnamon

1-cup blueberries, fresh or frozen

½ cup raisins

½ cup chopped hazelnuts (or any nuts of your choosing)

Splash of almond milk

Bring water to a boil in a small saucepan. Add quinoa, and return to a boil. Reduce heat to a simmer, covered, until most of the water has been absorbed.

Stir in sugar and cinnamon. Add raisins, blueberries and hazelnuts and cook for another minute. Let sit until desired thickness is reached. Serve with a splash of almond milk.

SIMPLE AVOCADO TOAST

Serves 2

4 Slices Sprouted Bread (I use Ezekiel), toasted

1 avocado, sliced

1 tsp. Olive Oil

Kosher Salt to taste

Sprinkle of crushed red pepper

Top toasted bread with the avocado. Mash and spread the avocado lightly onto the bread. Drizzle with olive oil. Sprinkle with salt and crushed red pepper.

HOMEMADE CHIA SEED PUDDING PARFAIT

Serves 2

2 cups unsweetened almond milk

½ tsp. vanilla extract

Pinch sea salt

4 tbsp. maple syrup

½ cup chia seeds

In a bowl, whisk almond milk, vanilla, salt, syrup, and chia seeds. Place in serving jugs and refrigerate for 2-3 hours, or overnight, until thick and cold. Stir to even out the consistency. Serve topped with your favorite fruits, nuts, raisins or granola. Enjoy!

ACAI BOWL

Serves 2

Two packets unsweetened frozen acai pulp (7 ounces)

1 medium banana

½ cup blueberries

½ cup strawberries

⅓ cup unsweetened almond milk

⅔ cup granola

1 tbsp. unsweetened coconut flakes

Drizzle of agave nectar or natural maple
syrup (optional)

2 tbsp. Whole hemp seeds (optional)

Break the frozen acai up my hitting the sealed packets against a hard surface or hitting them with a meat mallet. Blend it along with ⅔ the banana, ¼ cup of the blueberries and ¼ cup of the strawberries in the blender until a thick creamy mixture is achieved.

Slice the remaining banana strawberries. Arrange the slices and the remaining blueberries along with the granola and coconut flakes atop the acai. Drizzle agave or syrup and sprinkle with hemp seeds if desired. Enjoy!

STUFFED WARM APPLE

Serves 2

2 golden delicious apples

⅓-cup oatmeal or granola

¼ cup brown sugar

¼ tsp. cinnamon

Pinch of salt

Pinch nutmeg

2 Tsps. Earth Balance, divided

1-cup water

Preheat the oven to 350°. Core the apple almost all the way removing all seeds, but leaving enough for your filling not to spill through. Set aside.

In a medium bowl, mix all dry ingredients.

Fill apples with stuffing mix, packing it in tightly.

Set apples in a baking dish along with 1-cup of water, and place the Earth Balance atop each apple. Bake for 30 minutes. Remove from the oven and let cool about 5 minutes. Enjoy!

COLD MORNIN' OATMEAL

Serves 4

2 cups rolled oats

2 cups unsweetened almond milk

2 tbsp. raisins or other favorite dried fruit

½ tsp. vanilla extract

¼ cup of your favorite chopped nuts

2 apples, peaches or pears, pitted and sliced

2 tbsp. agave nectar

Combine oats, milk, and vanilla in a bowl. Cover and refrigerate overnight. In the morning, spoon a serving of the oatmeal into a serving dish and top with your favorite remaining ingredients, lastly drizzling with agave nectar.
Enjoy!

PLANTAIN PORRIDGE

Serves 6

About 1lb green plantains, washed peeled and sliced in 1-inch pieces

3 cups water

1 stick cinnamon bark

Pinch of salt

1 -cup coconut milk

1 tsp. vanilla extract

1 cup unsweetened almond milk

1 ½ tbsp. sugar

⅛ tsp. nutmeg

Place water and plantain in a blender and pulse until blended into a smooth puree. Pour the puree into a pot with cinnamon and turn on the stove to a low heat. Keep stirring to avoid clumping. Stir in salt. Add coconut milk and stir consistently for about 10-15 minutes. Add almond milk, vanilla, nutmeg and sugar, and continue to stir. Let cook an additional 20-25 minutes, constantly stirring. Let cool, and enjoy!

SOUPS AND SALADS

Curry Lentil Soup

Roasted Butternut Squash Soup

Vegan Chili

White Bean and Kale Soup

Black Bean Soup

Cream of Celery Soup

Carrot Ginger Soup

Vegetable Soup

Beet and Lentil Salad

Sweet Strawberry Arugula Salad

Couscous salad

Asian Cucumber Salad

Thai Noodle Salad

Simple Pasta Salad

Kale Salad

CURRY
LENTIL SOUP

Serves 4

1 tbsp. olive oil

1 large onion, chopped

2 cloves garlic, minced

4 medium carrots diced

1 2-lb bag butternut squash cut into ½ inch cubes

2 tsp. curry powder

1 tsp. ground cumin

¼ tsp. cayenne pepper

4 cups low sodium vegetable stock

½ not chicken bouillon cube

1 can coconut cream

1 can stewed tomatoes

1 18oz package steamed lentil

2 bay leaves

Sea salt and black pepper, to taste

In a stockpot, heat the olive oil over medium heat and stir-fry the onion and garlic until the onion is translucent, a couple of minutes.

Add carrots and butternut squash, curry powder, cumin and cayenne pepper and let brown, about a minute.

Add the vegetable stock, bouillon, coconut cream, stewed tomatoes and lentils. Cover and bring to a boil. Add bay leave, reduce the heat to low and allow to simmer for 20-30 minutes until butternut squash and carrots are tender. Season with a salt and pepper. Remove the bay leaves and enjoy!

VEGAN CHILI

Serves 6

1 tbsp. olive oil

½ cup diced onion

2 cloves garlic, minced

1 package vegan beef crumble or soyrizo

2 tbsp. chili powder

1 tsp. garlic powder

1 large tomato, diced

1 can tomato sauce

1 can kidney beans, well rinsed and drained

I can cannellini beans, rinsed and drained

½ can corn

Sea salt to taste

¼ cup pickled jalapenos, diced with a little of the juice

Sautee the onions, garlic and soyrizo over oil on low heat until onions become translucent. Season with chili powder and garlic powder. Add tomato, tomato sauce, kidney beans, cannellini beans, corn and jalapenos with juice. Let simmer on low for 10-15 minutes. Allow to cool and enjoy!

ROASTED BUTTERNUT SQUASH SOUP

Serves 4

1 2-lb bag butternut squash cut into
½ inch cubes
3 garlic cloves, peeled
2 small shallots, peeled and halved
½ sweet onion, peeled and quartered
1 tbsp. coconut oil
½ tsp. sea salt
2½ cups vegetable broth
Cayenne pepper to taste

Prepare vegetables, toss with olive oil on a roasting pan lined with parchment paper. Roast for 40 minutes, turning once, cooking until squash is tender. Remove and let cool for 15 minutes.

Place squash, shallots and onion in a blender and blend until creamy. Add to a pot with stock and salt. Cook on medium until heated through. Add cayenne pepper to taste, serve and enjoy!

WHITE BEAN AND KALE SOUP

Serves 6

1 lb. dried white beans, rinsed and picked over

¼ cup extra virgin olive oil

1 large yellow onion, chopped

2 celery stalks, chopped

2 large carrots, peeled and chopped

5 cloves garlic, minced

Salt and black pepper to taste

6 cups vegetable stock

One can diced tomatoes

3 fresh thyme sprigs

1 bay leaf

1 ½ lbs. kale

1 tbsp. soy sauce

Put the beans in a large pot and add enough water to cover them by 3 inches. Cover and bring to a boil, then reduce heat to a gentle simmer. Season with salt and cook, stirring occasionally until the beans are tender, 40 minutes- 2 hours depending on bean size. Drain and set aside to cool.

In a separate large pot over medium-high heat add olive oil. When it's hot, add onion, celery, carrot and garlic and season with salt and pepper. Cook, stirring frequently until the vegetable are soft, about 10-12 minutes. Add the drained beans along with the stock, tomatoes thyme and bay leaf. Stir, cover and bring to a boil. Adjust the heat so the soup simmers, and allow to cook for an additional 15 minutes.

Remove the thick stems and ribs from the kale and discard them. Roughly chop the leaves and stir into the soup along with soy sauce. Cover and cook until the kale is tender, about 10 minutes. Remove the thyme stems and bay leaf and adjust the seasoning as needed. Serve hot. Enjoy!

BLACK BEAN SOUP

Serves 4

2 tbsp. olive oil

2 medium yellow onions

4 celery ribs, chopped fine

2 large carrots, peeled and sliced into
thin rounds

6 cloves garlic, minced

4 tsps. ground cumin

½ tsp. red pepper flakes

4 cans organic black beans, rinsed
and drained

4 cups low sodium vegetable broth

1 ½ tbsp. sherry vinegar

Salt and pepper to taste

Optional Garnishes:

Sliced Avocado

Cilantro

Heat olive oil in a large stew pot until sizzling. Add onions, celery and carrot and a dash of salt. Cook, stirring occasionally until vegetables have softened, about 15 minutes.
Stir in the garlic, cumin and red pepper flakes and cook until fragrant, about a minute. Pour in the beans and broth and bring to a simmer. Cook until the broth is flavorful and the beans are very tender, about 30 minutes.

Remove soup from heat and allow to cool 5 minutes. Add about 4 cups of the soup to a blender and pulse until smooth, allowing steam to escape from the top of the blender to avoid burning. Return the pureed portion of the soup to the pot, simmer an additional 5 minutes. Add salt and pepper to taste and serve with garnish. Enjoy!

CREAM OF CELERY SOUP

Serves 4

1 tbsp. Earth Balance Vegan Spread

1 ½ tbsp. coconut oil

½ onion, chopped finely

½ bunch celery, cubed

1 small red potato, diced

1 bay leaf

2 cups vegetable broth

1-cup water

½ cup coconut cream

½ cup parsley, chopped

⅛ tsp. salt

Pepper to taste

In a large stockpot, add spread and oil to heat. Add onion, celery and potato. Sautee until tender, about 10 minutes.

Add broth, water, bay leaf, salt and pepper. Boil for 10 minutes. Reduce heat to a simmer, and add the coconut cream. Cook another 10-12 minutes.

Cool, remove bay leaf and add parsley. Put in blender and pulse until creamy, allowing steam and heat to escape from the lid to prevent burning (blend in batches to keep from making a mess or burning).

Place pureed mixture back into the pot and heat throughout. Season as needed. Enjoy!

CARROT GINGER SOUP

Serves 4

4 cups low-sodium vegetable broth

1 yellow onion, chopped

3 cloves garlic, finely chopped

2 tsp. freshly grated ginger

1 lb. carrots, peeled and coarsely chopped

1 medium yukon gold potato, peeled and chopped

In a large stockpot, add ½ cup of the broth and allow to heat. Add onion and garlic and cook until tender, about 5 minutes, stirring occasionally. Stir in ginger, carrots, potato and remaining broth and heat to a boil. Reduce to a simmer, cover and cook 25 minutes.

Cool, and pulse in a blender in 1 cup batches, returning each batch to the stock pot. Once fully blended, add salt and pepper as needed, heat 5 more minutes, and serve. Enjoy!

VEGETABLE SOUP

Serves 6

4 tbsp. olive oil

2 cups chopped leeks, white part only
(3 leeks)

2 tbsp. minced garlic

Kosher Salt to taste

2 cups carrots, peeled and chopped
into rounds

2 cups peeled and diced sweet potato

2 cups celery, washed and cubed

8 cups vegetable stock

4 cups peeled, seeded and chopped
tomatoes

1 can organic corn, drained and rinsed

1 bunch fresh kale, washed, stemmed
and chopped

½ tsp. black pepper

In a large stockpot, heat olive oil over medium-low heat. Once hot, add the leeks, garlic, and a pinch of salt and allow to brown. Add the carrots, potatoes and celery and allow to cook for 5 minutes, stirring occasionally.

Add the stock, increase the heat to high and bring to a simmer. Once simmering, add the tomatoes, corn, kale and pepper. Reduce heat to low, cover, and cook until the vegetables are tender, approximately 20-25 minutes. Remove from heat, season to taste with kosher salt, and serve immediately. Enjoy!

BEET AND LENTIL SALAD

Serves 6

8 oz. steamed lentils

8 oz. steamed and peeled beets, rinsed and cut into ¼ inch cubes

1 bag (7 oz.) fresh organic spinach

½ can organic corn, drained and rinsed

1 medium avocado, cut into small cubes

3 tbsp. olive oil

1 tbsp. apple cider vinegar

½ medium lime

Salt and pepper to taste

Sliced almonds to garnish

In a large bowl, combine lentils, beets, spinach, corn and avocado. Drizzle with olive oil and vinegar and squeeze lime over it. Add salt and pepper to taste. Mix until thoroughly coated. Top with sliced almond and serve. Enjoy!

SWEET STRAWBERRY ARUGULA SALAD

Serves 4

4 cups organic arugula

1 ½ cup quartered fresh strawberries

1 medium granny smith apple, peeled,
cored and sliced thinly

½ cup almonds

¼ small red onion, sliced finely

½ orange, freshly squeezed

4 tbsp. olive oil

2 tbsp. balsamic vinegar

⅛ tsp. ground ginger

Dash cayenne pepper

In a salad bowl, combine arugula, strawberries, apple, almonds and onion. In a small bowl, whisk together orange juice, oil, vinegar, ginger and cayenne pepper. Pour over salad, toss gently to coat, and serve. Enjoy!

COUSCOUS SALAD

Serves 6

1 cup vegetable broth

1 cup uncooked Israeli couscous

2 small sweet potatoes, peeled and cubed

1 tbsp. olive oil

½ sweet red pepper, seeded and diced

½ green pepper, seeded and diced

½ small red onion, finely sliced

1½ cup cherry tomatoes, halved

¼ leaf parsley

¼ cup sunflower seeds

½ cup dried cranberries

3 tbsp. olive oil

1 tbsp. grain mustard

1 tbsp. apple cider vinegar

1 tsp. dried oregano

¾ tsp. ground cumin

½ tsp. salt

½ tsp. pepper

Preheat oven to 400°.

When heated, add sweet potato and allow to roast until crisps, about 30-40 minutes.

In a small saucepan, bring broth to a boil. Add couscous. Allow to cook 5 minute, stirring occasionally. Remove from heat, cover and let stand, cool.

In a salad bowl, add peppers, onion, tomatoes, parsley, sunflower seeds and cranberries. Add roasted potatoes and cooled couscous.

In a small bowl, whisk together olive oil, mustard, vinegar, oregano, cumin salt and pepper.

Drizzle oil over salad and gently toss.

Serve immediately or refrigerate and serve cold. Enjoy!

ASIAN CUCUMBER SALAD

Serves 2

1 large cucumber, halved, seeded and sliced

1 large tomato, seeded and diced

1 avocado, cubed

1 tbsp. olive oil

1 tbsp. rice vinegar

½ tbsp. toasted sesame seeds

Salt and pepper to taste

In a bowl add cucumber, tomato and avocado. In a separate bowl, whisk together olive oil, vinegar, sesame seeds, salt and pepper.

Drizzle over salad and toss. Enjoy!

THAI NOODLE SALAD

Serves 2

6 oz. rice noodles

Dressing:

½ cup chunky peanut butter

3 tbsp. soy sauce

3 tbsp. Sriracha sauce

2 tbsp. fresh lime juice

2 tbsp. rice vinegar

1 tbsp. sesame oil

1 clove garlic, minced

1 tbsp. brown sugar

3 tbsp. warm water

Salad:

2 medium bell peppers, sliced into strips (red, orange, yellow)

1 large cucumber, seeded, quartered and cubed

½ cup shredded carrots

½ cup bean sprouts

1 cup fresh cilantro

6 scallions, diced

2 jalapeño peppers, seeded and cut into fine strips

Red pepper flakes to taste

Cook noodles as directed on packaging. Drain and transfer to a large bowl of ice water. Separate noodles until thoroughly chilled. Set aside.

In a large bowl, combine peanut butter, soy sauce, Sriracha sauce, lime juice, vinegar, sesame oil, garlic, sugar and water. Whisk until thoroughly combined.

Drain noodles, and add to bowl. Add bell peppers, cucumbers, carrots, bean sprouts, cilantro, scallions and jalapeños. Toss to combine. Serve immediately, red pepper flakes. Enjoy!

KALE SALAD

Serves 4

1 bunch kale, stemmed and finely chopped

¼ cup olive oil

¼ cup grapefruit juice

2 tbsp. apple cider vinegar

1 avocado, cut into small cubes

8 oz. beets, steamed and peeled and cut into small cubes

3 tbsp. dried currants

¼ cup sliced almonds

½ apple, peeled and cored and sliced thinly

1 ½ cup Julianne carrots

In a large salad bowl, combine kale, olive oil, grapefruit juice, vinegar and avocado. With hand mix and massage until thoroughly coated and leaves are softened. Add in remaining ingredients, and allow to sit for at least 30 minutes, allowing the kale toe soften. Serve and enjoy!

SIMPLE PASTA SALAD

Serves 4

10 oz. penne or bowtie pasta

2 cups frozen peas, steamed

1 cup fresh basil, chopped finely

3 oz. sun dried tomato

1 tsp. garlic powder

¼ cup olive oil

Salt and pepper to taste

Cook pasta as directed on packaging. Simultaneously, steam frozen peas in another pot. Drain and rinse both. Add peas to pasta, along with basil, sun fried tomato and garlic powder. Drizzle with olive oil and add salt and pepper to taste. Toss. Enjoy!

FAVES

Stuffed Shells

Roasted Veggies

Black Eyed Peas Shepard's Pie

Avocado Pistachio Pesto Pasta

Lasagna

Peanut Noodle Salad

Sweet Potato Fries

Lentil Loaf

Brussels Sprouts Pasta

Arroz con habichuela Roja

Mushroom Risotto with Caramelized Onions

Chickpea Salad Sandwich

STUFFED SHELLS

Serves 6

8 oz. vegan jumbo pasta shells

15 oz. lentils

1 ½ cup Hazelnut ricotta (*see page 126*)

8 oz. Frozen spinach, thawed and patted dry

1 jar (25oz.) marinara sauce

Cook shells in salted boiling water until barely tender, about 12 minutes. Drain and cool until cold water. Drain again. Set aside.

Preheat oven to 350°. In a large bowl, combine lentils, ricotta and spinach.

Spread half the marinara over the bottom of the baking dish to coat it. Spoon a heaping tablespoon of filling into each shell and places the open side up in the dish, packing them into the dish tightly in a single layer. Pour remaining marinara evenly over the shells and sprinkle with mozzarella. Bake until cheese is melted and sauce is bubbling, about 30-35 minutes. Enjoy!

Drizzle over salad and toss. Enjoy!

ROASTED VEGGIES

Serves 6

1 head cauliflower, cut into medium sized florets, discarding stems

1 2-lb bag butternut squash cut into ½ inch cubes

1 lb. Brussels sprouts, washed and halved

1 large green apple, seeded and cut into cubes

2 tbsp. olive oil

1 tsp. rosemary

Salt and pepper to taste

1 tbsp. maple syrup

Preheat oven to 400°.

Line a baking dish with parchment paper. Add cauliflower, squash, brussels sprouts and apples. Toss in olive oil, rosemary, salt and pepper and maple syrup. Bake uncovered for 30-35 minutes. Allow to cool. Enjoy!

BLACK EYED PEAS SHEPARD'S PIE

Serves 6

Filling:

1 ½ cups black eyed peas

1 tbsp. olive oil

1 large onion, chopped

3 cloves garlic, crushed

2 sticks celery, chopped

1 carrot, chopped

1 zucchini, chopped

2 cup pumpkin, cubed

3 cups vegetable stock

2 tsp. oregano

1 tsp. dried thyme

2 bay leaves

Fresh parsley, handful, chopped

I can chopped tomatoes

2 tbsp. Vegan Worcestershire sauce

1 tbsp. tomato paste

Cauliflower Mash Topping:

1 head cauliflower

1 cup unsweetened coconut milk

2 cloves garlic, chopped

½ tsp. sea salt

½ tsp. black pepper

1 tsp. paprika

1 tbsp. olive oil

The night before, rinse the beans under cold water and allow to soak overnight in cold water.

Preheat oven to 425°. Wash cauliflower and cut into medium sized florets, discarding stems. Place cauliflower on parchment paper lined baking sheet. Drizzle with garlic, olive oil, a pinch of sea salt and pepper. Roast for 20 minutes until slightly browned.

Reduce heat to 350°.

Place roasted cauliflower, garlic, coconut milk, remainder of salt and pepper into blender or food processor and puree.

In the meantime, rinse the beans under water and add them to a large pot of boiling water with a pinch of salt. Cook for 1 hour.

In a saucepan over medium heat, add oil. When hot, add onion and garlic and allow to brown. Add beans, celery, carrots, zucchini, pumpkin, stock, herbs, tomatoes, Worcestershire sauce, salt and pepper. Simmer for 30 minutes.

In a casserole dish, add the bean and tomato mix and top with garlic mash. Bake 40 minutes until slightly brown at the top. Enjoy!

AVOCADO PISTACHIO PESTO PASTA

Serves 4

1 lb. vegan pasta of your choice

2 ripe avocados, seeded and diced

1 ½ cup roasted, salted pistachio nuts

1 cup fresh basil

4 cloves garlic

Zest and juice of one lemon

1 tsp. salt

Up to ¼ cup warm water

Chopped sun dried tomatoes

Cook pasta according to package directions.

Add avocado, 1 cup of pistachio nuts, basil, garlic, lemon zest and juice, salt water (amount varies based on desired consistency) to a blender and blend until very smooth.

Toss the pesto sauce with the pasta, sundried tomatoes and remaining pistachios. Serve and Enjoy!

PEANUT NOODLE SALAD

Serves 4

2 large cucumbers, peeled

1 cup soy sauce

½ cup coconut milk

½ cup rice wine vinegar

½ cup chunky peanut butter

4 cloves garlic, minced

1 tsp. sesame oil

1 tsp. red pepper flakes

½ tsp. salt

16 oz. soba noodles, cooked

6 oz. julienned carrots

6 green onions, sliced into ½ inch pieces

Cook pasta according to package directions.

Cut cucumbers half lengthwise and remove the seeds. Cut into half-moons pieces about ½ inch thick.

In a bowl, whisk together soy sauce, coconut milk, vinegar, peanut butter, garlic, sesame oil, red pepper flakes and salt. Add pasta, cucumber, carrots and green onions. Toss to evenly coat. Chill about 4 hours. Serve and enjoy!

LASAGNA

Serves 8-12

1 package of vegan no boil lasagna noodles

1 ½ cup Hazelnut ricotta
(see page 126)

1 package "beef" crumbles

1 tbsp. olive oil

¼ tsp. sea salt

⅛ tsp. black pepper

¼ tsp. garlic powder

1 tbsp. ketchup

1 bag fresh spinach

1 package Daiya© mozzarella shreds
(½ cup separated)

4 tbsp. Bread Crumbs

Fresh basil for garnish

1 Jar Marinara sauce

Preheat oven to 350°.

Prepare the hazelnut ricotta as directed. Set aside.

In a large skillet, heat olive oil. When hot, add beef crumbles, salt, pepper, garlic powder and ketchup. Allow to brown and heat thoroughly. Drain set aside.

Ladle some marinara in a 9x12 baking dish. Place noodles on the marinara to cover the bottom of the dish. Spoon half of the ricotta cheese over the noodles evenly. Next, spoon half of the "beef" crumbles over the ricotta. Add ½ of the spinach evenly then half of the Daiya mozzarella. Top with more marinara sauce.

Add a second layer of lasagna noodles, followed by remaining ricotta, remaining "beef" crumbles, remaining spinach, the other half of the Daiya mozzarella, and a few ladles of marinara.

Add the final layer of noodles. Top with separated Daiya mozzarella and a few more ladles of marinara. Sprinkle bread crumbs over the top of the dish.

Cover the dish with foil and bake 45-60 minutes. Remove the foil and bake an additional 15 minutes until the noodles have softened, the cheese has melted, and the sauce bubbles.

Remove the lasagna from the oven and let it sit and set about 15 minutes. Garnish with fresh basil and Enjoy!

SWEET POTATO FRIES

Serves 2-4

4 sweet potatoes, peeled and cut into thin wedges

4 tbsp. olive oil

½ tsp. garlic powder

Salt and pepper to taste

Preheat over to 425°.

In a large mixing bowl, combine potato wedges, olive oil, garlic powder, salt and pepper. Mix until evenly coated.

Add potatoes to a baking dish, arranges in a single layer. Bake for 15 minutes, and then flip the fries to cook on the other side. Bake an additional 12-15 minutes. Enjoy!

LENTIL LOAF

Serves 6

1 cup dry lentils (green or brown)

2 ½ cups vegetable broth

3 tbsp. flaxseed meal

⅓ cup water

2 tbsp. olive oil

3 cloves garlic, minced

1 small onion, diced

1 small red bell pepper, seeded and diced

4 stalks celery

1 carrot, grated

1 tsp. dried thyme

½ tsp. cumin

½ tsp. garlic powder

½ tsp. onion powder

salt and pepper to taste

¾ cup oats

½ cup oat flour

1 ½ tbsp. brown mustard

2 tbsp. ketchup

Glaze:

3 tbsp. ketchup

1 tbsp. balsamic vinegar

1 tbsp. maple syrup

1 tbsp. Nutritional yeast

Rinse lentils. In a large pot, add 2 ½ cups broth with lentils and bring to a boil. Reduce heat and allow to simmer, about 45 minutes, stirring occasionally.

Preheat oven to 350°.

In a small bowl, combine flaxseed meal and water. Whisk thoroughly and let sit 10 minutes.

In a sauté pan, heat oil over medium heat. Add garlic, onion, pepper, carrots, celery, thyme, cumin, garlic powder, onion powder and salt and pepper, and allow to cook until onions become translucent.

In a blender or food processor, blend ¾ lentil mixture until thick paste is achieved.

In a large bowl, add blended lentil mixture, flaxseed meal mixture, sautéed vegetables, oats, oat flour, ketchup and mustard. Mix well.

Line a baking dish with parchment paper and place the mixture into the dish, molding and patting it down into a loaf.

In a small bowl, add the ketchup, vinegar and maple syrup for the glaze. Whisk well, and distribute evenly over the loaf. Sprinkle the top of the loaf with nutritional yeast.

Bake in the oven for about 45-55 minutes. Let cool, and Enjoy!

BRUSSELS SPROUTS PASTA

Serves 4

8 oz. vegan pasta of your choice

2 tbsp. Earth Balance

¼ cup panko

2 tbsp. olive oil

12 oz. Brussels sprouts, quartered

2 medium shallots, thinly sliced

1 clove garlic, minced

⅔ cups vegetable broth

½ tsp. thyme

Salt and pepper to taste

2 tbsp. chopped pistachios, pine nuts or hazelnuts

2 tbsp. nutritional yeast

Cook pasta according to package directions.

In a skillet, melt Earth Balance over medium heat. Add panko and cook 3 minutes until brown, taking care to stir frequently. Set aside.

In another skillet, heat olive oil over medium heat. Add Brussels sprouts and cook 3 minutes. Add shallots and garlic and let cook until shallots and Brussels sprouts begin to brown. Add vegetable broth, thyme, salt and pepper. Cover and cook an additional 3 minutes.

Add Brussels sprouts mixture to pasta and toss well. Sprinkle with nuts, panko, and nutritional yeast and serve immediately. Enjoy!

ARROZ CON HABICHUELA ROJA

Serves 4

2 cups grain rice, rinsed of it's starch (this is important)

4-5 cups water

½ cup sofrito

16 oz. pigeon peas

1 tbsp. chopped black olives

1 tbsp. capers

1 packet Sazon with achiote

1 can tomato sauce

3 tbsp. olive oil

salt and pepper to taste

In a medium sized deep pot, heat the olive oil. Add tomato sauce, olives, capers, sofrito and sazon. Cook over medium heat about 5 minutes. Add all other ingredients and enough water that it's 1 inch over the rice line.

Bring to a boil and cook over high heat until most of the water is absorbed. Once the water has been absorbed, stir gently once. Cover and turn the heat to low. Cook another 30 minutes or until the rice is tender.

MUSHROOM RISOTTO WITH CARAMELIZED ONIONS

Serves 4

2 cups butternut squash

½ cup canned coconut milk

5 sage leaves

3-4 yellow onions

4 tbsp. olive oil, plus 1 tbsp.

4 cloves garlic, minced

¾ lb. cremini mushrooms, sliced

1 large fresh sprig rosemary

1 cup uncooked quinoa

2 tbsp. balsamic vinegar

½ cup dry white wine

2 ½ cups vegetable broth

2 tsp. salt

½ tsp. black pepper

1 tbsp. Earth Balance

Place butternut squash in a dish lines with parchment paper. Drizzle with 1 tbsp. of olive oil and place in the oven for 30-45 minutes. Remove from the oven and allow to cool. Place in a blender with coconut milk and sage and process until smooth.

Chop 2 small onions. In a large skillet, heat 1 tbsp. olive oil over medium heat. Cook onion about 5 minutes, stirring frequently. Add the garlic and cook 5 more minutes.

Turn the heat up to medium-high and add mushrooms. Cook another 7-10 minutes.

Add the rosemary, ½ tsp. of the salt and pepper, taking care to stir well. Cook a few more minutes. Add in the quinoa, balsamic vinegar and broth and stir. Bring to a boil. Cover the pan. Make sure the check and stir every few minutes, reducing heat if necessary to avoid burning.

In a separate skillet, heat 3 tbsp. olive oil. Cut the remaining onions in half, then into thin crescent-moons. Add them to the oil and sprinkle with remaining salt. Cook on low heat, stirring occasionally, until the onion turn a dark brown color, about 30 minutes. Keep an eye on this to prevent burning.

When the quinoa mixture has finished cooking, remove the rosemary sprig and stir in the butternut squash puree plus a spoonful of Earth Balance. Stir until well combined and the puree is heated throughout. Serve topped with caramelized onions. Enjoy!

CHICKPEA SALAD SANDWICH

Serves 2

1 can chickpeas, drained and rinsed

2 stalks celery, finely chopped

2 tbsp. sweet relish

¼ cup chopped red bell pepper

3 tbsp. vegan mayonnaise

1 clove garlic

1 ½ tbsp. mustard

Juice of ¼ lime

Salt and pepper to taste

4 slices Sprouted Bread or 2 spinach wraps

In a large bowl, mash the chickpeas with a potato masher until a nice combination of creamy and chunky in consistency.

Stir in celery, relish, bell pepper, mayonnaise, garlic, mustard and lime juice until combined. Add salt and pepper to taste. Serve with toasted sprouted bread or rolled in wraps. Enjoy!

HOLIDAY

Creamy Mac and Cheese

Green Bean Casserole

Quinoa and Peas

Sweet Potato

Homemade Cranberry Sauce

Potato Salad

Caramelized Brussels Sprouts

Collard Greens

Brown Sugar Carrots

Cauliflower Mash with Gravy

New Year's Black Eyed Peas

CREAMY MAC AND CHEESE

Serves 8-10

¼ cup raw cashews

¾ cup water

2 cloves garlic

2 tbsp. nutritional yeast

1 tbsp. fresh lemon juice

½ tsp. onion powder

½ tsp. smoked paprika

¼ tsp. chili powder

1 tsp. sea salt

⅛ tsp. liquid smoke

hot sauce to taste

1 package vegan macaroni

6 tablespoons Earth Balance spread

2 cups Daiya© pepper jack-style cheese, ½ cup separated

2 cups Daiya cheddar-style cheese, ½ cup separated

1 ½ cup almond milk

½ cup vegan breadcrumbs

Place cashews in a small bowl, cover with water and allow to soak overnight or for at least 4 hours.

Preheat oven to 425° and line baking sheet with parchment paper. Spread out squash on sheet and drizzle with oil. Toss to coat. Sprinkle with salt. Roast for 20 minutes. Flip and roast for another 20 minutes until fork tender. Let cool.

Reduce oven temperature to 350°.

Add the soaked cashews, water, nutritional yeast, lemon juice, onion powder, paprika, chili powder and 2 cups of the cooked squash into a high-speed blender. Blend on high until smooth. Add salt, liquid smoke and hot sauce to taste and blend again.

Cook pasta according to package directions.

Add drained pasta back into the pot and turn heat on medium.

Pour on your desired amount of sauce and stir to combine. Stir in Earth Balance and stir until it begins to melt. Add Daiya cheeses (excluding removed portions) and almond milk. Allow to heat through until cheese becomes gooey and melted and creamy.

Transfer dish to a baking pan and distribute evenly. Top with remaining cheese and breadcrumbs evenly. Cover with foil and bake for 30-40 minutes until cheese begins to bubble. Allow to cool. Enjoy!

GREEN BEAN CASSEROLE

Serves 8-10

2 cups fresh green beans, washed and snapped of its ends

2 cups vegetable stock

1 tbsp. olive oil

1 onion, diced

2 cloves garlic, minced

Salt and pepper to taste

1 ½ cup Hazelnut ricotta *(see page 126)*

1 ½ cups Daiya cheddar-style cheese,

1 cup separated

I package crispy fried onions

Preheat oven to 350°.

In a large stockpot, heat olive oil. Add onion, garlic, salt and pepper, and allow to brown. When onion becomes translucent, add stock and green beans and bring to a boil.

Turn heat to low and cover, allowing the liquid to almost completely evaporate.

Transfer the green beans from the pot to a baking dish. Stir in Hazelnut Ricotta and half of the Daiya cheese. Top with remaining Daiya cheese. Top with crispy fried onions. Cover and bake 25-30 minutes. Enjoy!

QUINOA AND PEAS

Serves 8-10

2 cups Quinoa

1 can kidney beans, rinsed and drained

2 sprigs thyme

2 cloves garlic

2 stalks green onion

1 tsp. sugar

1 whole green pepper (scotch bonnet or habanero)

1 can coconut cream

2-4 tbsp. coconut oil

1 tsp. baking soda

2 tsp. salt

Preheat oven to 350°.

In a large pot, add 4 cups of water and beans, bring to a boil. Cover and reduce to a simmer, about 3-4 hours. When the beans are tender, add coconut cream. Cook for until soft, then add thyme, green onions, sugar, salt, whole pepper, coconut oil and quinoa. Stir. Bring to a boil and reduce heat and cook on low heat. Quinoa should begin to thicken and all the liquid should be absorbed. Stir, taking care not to puncture the pepper. Remove from heat, and keep covered allowing the quinoa and beans to continue to cook throughout. Let cool. Enjoy!

SWEET POTATO

Serves 8-10

2 ½ lbs. sweet potatoes, peeled sliced

2 tbsp. olive oil

3 tbsp. Earth Balance

3 tbsp. packed dark brown sugar, divided

1 tsp. sea salt

½ tsp. ground cinnamon

½ tsp. ginger

Pinch nutmeg

Black pepper to taste

¼ cup chopped pecans

½ cup rolled oats

2 tbsp. coconut oil

2 tbsp. pure maple syrup

2 cups vegan marshmallows

Preheat oven to 400°.

Place the sweet potatoes on a baking sheet. Drizzle with olive oil and bake for 40-50 minutes. Remove from oven place in a large mixing bowl.

Mash the potatoes until smooth. Add half of the Earth Balance, half of the brown sugar, salt, cinnamon, ginger, nutmeg and black pepper. Whisk the mixture until smooth.

Coat a baking dish with remaining Earth Balance. Pour the sweet potato mixture into the pan.

In a food processor, chop pecans and rolled oats. Place in a bowl and use a fork to mix with coconut oil and maple syrup and remaining brown sugar until a crumble mixture is formed.

Sprinkle the nut/oat topping mixture atop the sweet potato evenly. Top with marshmallows.

Bake uncovered for 15-25 minutes until the dish is hot throughout and the toppings browns. Enjoy!

HOMEMADE CRANBERRY SAUCE

Serves 8-10

8 medium red potatoes, scrubbed and diced

4 celery ribs, washed and diced

½ red pepper, diced

½ green pepper, diced

½ orange pepper, diced

1 small onion, minced

¾ cup veganaise

3 tbsp. mustard

1 tsp. salt

1 tsp. garlic powder

½ tsp. black pepper

1 tbsp. sweet relish

Paprika to taste

Boil potatoes in salted water until fork tender. Drain and allow to cool to room temperature.

In a large bowl, add potatoes, celery, peppers and onions, veganaise, mustard, salt, garlic powder, black pepper and sweet relish. Mix until evenly distributed. Garnish with a few dashed of paprika. Enjoy!

POTATO SALAD

Serves 8-10

8 medium red potatoes, scrubbed and diced

4 celery ribs, washed and diced

½ red pepper, diced

½ green pepper, diced

½ orange pepper, diced

1 small onion, minced

¾ cup veganaise

3 tbsp. mustard

1 tsp. salt

1 tsp. garlic powder

½ tsp. black pepper

1 tbsp. sweet relish

Paprika to taste

Boil potatoes in salted water until fork tender. Drain and allow to cool to room temperature.

In a large bowl, add potatoes, celery, peppers and onions, veganaise, mustard, salt, garlic powder, black pepper and sweet relish. Mix until evenly distributed. Garnish with a few dashed of paprika. Enjoy!

CARAMELIZED BRUSSELS SPROUTS

Serves 4-6

2 tbsp. olive oil

3 cups fresh Brussels sprouts, halved

2 large shallots, chopped

2 tbsp. sliced almonds

½ tsp. sea salt

Heat skillet over medium-high heat. Add sliced almonds and toast for about 3-5 minutes until golden brown and fragrant. Remove from pan and set aside.

Add 1 tbsp. olive oil and shallots to pan and cook until caramelized and browned on the edges. Remove shallots and set aside. Add 1 tbsp. olive oil to hot pan and add Brussels Sprouts, cut sides facing down. Cook 5-7 minutes, and when caramelized, turn over and cook an additional 5 minutes. Add onions to Brussels sprouts, and stir to combine. Top with toasted sliced almonds and sea salt. Enjoy!

CAULIFLOWER MASH WITH GRAVY

Serves 4-6

Cauliflower Mash:

1 head cauliflower

1 cup unsweetened coconut milk

2 cloves garlic, chopped

½ tsp. sea salt

½ tsp. black pepper

1 tbsp. olive oil

Gravy:

1 cup vegetable broth

¼ cup nutritional yeast

1 tsp. yellow mustard

1 tbsp. tamari

1 large garlic clove, minced

1 tbsp. cornstarch

2 tbsp. tahini

1 ½ tbsp. balsamic vinegar

½ tsp. maple syrup

2 tbsp. olive oil

Preheat oven to 425°.

Wash cauliflower and cut into medium sized florets, discarding stems. Place cauliflower on parchment paper lined baking sheet. Drizzle with garlic, olive oil, a pinch of sea salt and pepper. Roast for 20 minutes until slightly browned.

Place roasted cauliflower, garlic, coconut milk, remainder of salt and pepper into blender or food processor and puree. You may have to do this in portions depending on the size of your blender. Place in a serving dish.

In a blender combine all the vegetable broth, nutritional yeast, mustard, tamari, garlic, cornstarch, tahini, vinegar, syrup and olive oil and puree until smooth. Transfer to a medium pot and heat on low until it comes to a boil. Reduce heat to low and stir frequently until desired thickness is achieved. Place in a serving gravy bowl. Enjoy!

COLLARD GREENS

Serves 8-10

2 tbsp. olive oil

1 large yellow onion, halved and thinly sliced

1 not-beef cube

1 tsp. crushed red chili flakes

3 cloves garlic, chopped

1 tbsp. smoked paprika

¼ tsp. fine sea salt

½ tsp. ground black pepper

1 tsp. liquid smoke

2 bunches greens, washed thoroughly, stemmed and sliced into 2-inch parts

4 cups vegetable stock

Heat a large high-sided skillet over medium heat. When the pan is very hot, add olive oil and allow to heat. Add onion, not-beef cube, red chili flakes, garlic, paprika, salt, pepper and liquid smoke and cook until onion becomes translucent. Slowly add in greens and stir over the heat for 2 minutes. Stir in vegetable stock and bring to a boil. Allow to boil for 5 minutes, before reducing the heat to a simmer. Allow to simmer, 2-4 hours, adding more stock or water as needed until the leaves are dark and very tender. Enjoy!

BROWN SUGAR CARROTS

Serves 8-10

2 tbsp. extra-virgin olive oil

1 ½ pounds baby carrots with the tops still on, peeled

Salt and Pepper to taste

2 tbsp. packed light-brown sugar

1 tbsp. molasses

1 ½ tbsp. Earth Balance

Pinch rosemary

Heat oil in a large skillet over medium heat. Add carrots and season with salt and pepper. Add oil and stir to coat. Allow to cook 3 minutes. Add brown sugar and molasses, stir to coat. Cook until carrots are tender and sauce has thickened, about 5 minutes. Add Earth Balance and rosemary to skillet and cook until butter is melted.

Transfer carrots to a serving dish. Enjoy!

NEW YEAR'S BLACK EYED PEAS

Serves 4-6

1 tbsp. olive oil

1 large onion, chopped

1 large green bell pepper, chopped

2 stalks celery, chopped

4 garlic cloves, minced

½ tsp. crushed red pepper

¼ tsp. smoked paprika

4 allspice berries

1 not beef bouillon cube

1 tsp. liquid smoke

2 ½ cups blacked eyed peas (canned or frozen)

6 cups veggie stock

1 tsp. dried thyme or 3 fresh sprigs

4 bay leaves

sea salt and black pepper to taste

Heat olive oil in a large soup pot on medium fire. When hot, add onion, green pepper, celery, garlic, crushed red pepper, paprika, allspice berries and bouillon and allow to cook until veggies become soft and fragrant. Add in liquid smoke and stir.

Add in peas, veggie stock, thyme, bay leaves, salt and pepper. Stir, then lower flame and allow to cook on low heat for 45-60 minutes. Enjoy!

In a blender combine all the vegetable broth, nutritional yeast, mustard, tamari, garlic, cornstarch, tahini, vinegar, syrup and olive oil and puree until smooth. Transfer to a medium pot and heat on low until it comes to a boil. Reduce heat to low and stir frequently until desired thickness is achieved. Place in a serving gravy bowl. Enjoy!

DESSERTS

Warm Apple Pie

Blueberry Crumble

Old Fashioned Pumpkin Pie

Vegan Cornbread

Brownies

Blueberry Cheesecake

Homemade Chocolate Banana Peanut Butter Ice Cream

Homemade Strawberry Ice cream

Chocolate Chip Cookies

WARM APPLE PIE

Serves 8

2 dairy-free traditional flour piecrusts, room temperature

¾ cup sugar

3 tbsp. all-purpose flour

1 tsp. cinnamon

¼ tsp. ground ginger

⅛ tsp. kosher salt

4 lbs. mixed apples, peeled, cored and cut into thin slices

4 tsp. fresh lemon juice

2 Tbsp. Earth Balance, divided

1 Flaxseed Egg Replacement* *(see page 127)*

Preheat oven to 425°.

In a large bowl, combine sugar, flour, cinnamon, ginger and salt. Add apples and lemon juice. Gently toss to combine until evenly coated. Place filling in one of the pie crusts, then dot with Earth Balance. Cover with other pie crust and gently press edges to seal. Cut a large X into the top and gently pull back the corners of the X to allow steam to escape.

In a small egg, prepare 1 flaxseed egg replacement as instructed. Brush the "egg" mixture onto the crust.

Place the pie on a baking sheet lined with foil and bake for 15 minutes. Reduce heat to 375° and continue baking until bubbles occur and the crust is golden, about an hour. Cool on a wire rack for 1 hour allowing to set. Enjoy!

OLD FASHIONED PUMPKIN PIE

1-15oz. can pumpkin puree

1 ½ cup almond milk

½ cup dark brown sugar

⅓ cup white sugar

½ tsp. salt

4 tbsp. cornstarch

2 tsp. cinnamon

1 tsp. ginger

¼ tsp. nutmeg

¼ tsp. ground cloves

½ tsp. lemon zest

1 vegan graham cracker piecrust

Preheat oven to 425°.

In a large bowl, combine all ingredients, beating until everything is very well mixed. Pour the filling into the piecrust. Bake for 15 minutes. Lower the temperature to 350° and bake an additional 45-55 minutes, until knife inserted comes out clean. Allow to cool on a wire rack for two hours. Serve and Enjoy!

BLUEBERRY CRUMBLE

Serves 8

½ cup all-purpose flour

½ cup firmly packed brown sugar

½ teaspoon ground cinnamon

4 tbsps. Earth Balance, divided

¼ cup granulated sugar

¼ cup all-purpose flour

4 cups fresh blueberries, picked over

½ teaspoon finely grated lemon rind

1 tbsp. fresh lemon juice

2 Tbsp. Earth Balance, divided

Preheat oven to 400°.

In a medium bowl, stir together the flour, brown sugar and cinnamon until well blended. Work Earth Balance in with a fork or your fingertips until mixture resembles crumbs the size of small peas. Set aside.

In a large bowl, stir together sugar and flour until well mixed. Gently stir in blueberries, lemon rind and lemon juice. Pour mixture into piecrust, then dot top with remaining butter.

Sprinkle crumb topping evenly over top of pie. Reduce oven temperature to 350°; place pie in oven and bake until topping is golden brown, 40 to 45 minutes. Remove to a wire rack; let cool completely before serving. Enjoy!

VEGAN CORNBREAD

2 cups cornmeal

1 cup organic unbleached all-purpose flour

2 tsp. baking powder

¼ tsp. Sea salt

2 cups non-dairy milk (room temperature)

⅓ cup melted vegan butter

4 tbsp. organic maple syrup

Preheat oven to 350˚

Combine all dry ingredients together in a medium-sized bowl and stir until well combined. Add in milk, melted butter and syrup and mix with a wooden spoon, gently.

Transfer the mixture to an 8 x 8 baking pan lined with parchment paper and spread evenly.

Bake at 350˚ for approximately 30-35 minutes, or until the top is golden. Enjoy!

HOMEMADE CHOCOLATE BANANA PEANUT BUTTER ICE CREAM

Serves 2

2 large frozen bananas- sliced

2 tbsp. cocoa powder

3 tbsp. creamy natural peanut butter

½ tsp. vanilla

¼ tsp. cinnamon

pinch salt

Place all ingredients in a high-speed blender or food processor and pulse slowly, scraping down the sides as you go, until mixture is creamy and smooth. This may take several minutes. Serve immediately or freeze in an airtight container for up to 5 days.

CHOCOLATY BROWNIES

Serves 8-12

1 ½ cup flour

1 ¼ cup sugar

½ coco powder

½ cup unsweetened coconut milk

½ cup coconut oil

1 ½ tsp. vanilla

¼ tsp. baking soda

½ cup chopped walnuts

pinch of salt

¼ cup coconut flakes (optional)

Preheat oven to 350°.

In a large mixing bowl, combine flour, coco powder, baking soda and salt. Mix well. Add in sugar, coconut milk, oil and vanilla and whisk until thoroughly combined. Fold in walnuts.

Line an 8x8 baking dish with parchment paper, and add the mix.

Top with an even distribution of coconut flakes.

Bake about 25 minutes until toothpick inserted comes out clean. Allow to cool, and enjoy!

BLUEBERRY CHEESECAKE

Serves 8

1 graham cracker pie crust

Filling:

1 cup cashews, soaked 3-5 hours

¼ cup unsweetened almond milk

2 tbsp. coconut oil

1 tsp. vanilla extract

1 tbsp. maple syrup

Zest of ¼ lemon

Blueberry Topping:

2 cups fresh blueberries

2 tbsp. maple syrup

Juice from ½ lemon

Allow the cashews to soak in a bowl of warm water for 3-5 hours.

In a blender or food processor, combine soaked cashews, almond milk, coconut oil, vanilla, syrup and lemon zest, and blend until a smooth puree is formed. Set aside.

Spoon filling mixture into the pie crust and evenly distribute. Cover the crust with plastic wrap and place in the freezer.

To make the topping, put a small saucepan over low-medium heat. Add in blueberries, syrup and lemon juice and stir occasionally with a wooden spoon until the blueberries begin to swell and break. Use the back of your spoon to help break any stubborn blueberries, and continue to cook until the mixture begins to simmer. Remove from heat and allow to cool five minutes before putting the mixture in a blender. Blend until smooth. Set aside and allow to cool fully.

Remove the cashew mixture filled pie crust from the freezer, and top with blueberry topping, spreading to evenly distribute. Cover again with plastic wrap and place back in the freezer. Chill for about 4 hours until firm.

To serve, allow to thaw about 5-10 minutes on the counter, and enjoy!

HOMEMADE STRAWBERRY ICE CREAM

Serves 2

2 cans full-fat coconut milk (refrigerated overnight)

2 cups frozen strawberries

2 tsp. maple syrup

½ tsp. vanilla extract

Open the cans of coconut milk and spoon out the top thick white layer, add to blender (the remaining liquid can be used in smoothies later!). Add strawberries, syrup and vanilla to the blender and pulse slowly, scraping down the sides as you go, until mixture is creamy and smooth. This may take several minutes. Serve immediately or freeze in an airtight container for up to 5 days.

CHOCOLATE CHIP COOKIES

Yields 8-12 cookies

½ cup coconut oil

1 cup brown sugar

¼ cup almond milk

1 tbsp. vanilla extract

2 cups flour

1 tsp. baking soda

1 tsp. baking powder

1 cup vegan chocolate chips

Pinch of salt

Preheat oven to 350°.

In a large bowl, combine coconut oil and brown sugar. Next, add in almond milk and vanilla. Thoroughly mix.

In a separate bowl, mix together flour, baking soda, baking powder and salt.

Add the wet mixture to the dry mixture bowl and mix well before folding in the chocolate chips.

The texture should be pretty crumbly. Roll into tablespoon sized balls and place them on an ungreased cookie sheet, making sure to flatten them slightly with your palm.

Line entire baking sheet with "cookie balls", leaving an inch of space between each.

Bake for 7-10 minutes. Allow to cool, and enjoy!

EXTRA

Hazelnut Ricotta

Vegan Parmesan Cheese

Coconut Whipped Cream

Flax Egg Replacement

HAZELNUT RICOTTA

Yields 2 cups

1 ½ cup hazelnuts, soaked at least 4 hours

½ cup water

Juice of ½ lemon

2 cloves garlic, diced

2 tbsp. extra virgin olive oil

½ tsp. kosher salt

2 ½ tbsp. nutritional yeast

2 tbsp. fresh parsley, minced

2 tbsp. fresh basil, minced

Add all ingredients to a food processor or high-powered blender and pulse until but all fully ground, making sure to scrape the sides until entire mixture is smooth.

VEGAN PARMESAN CHEESE

Yields 1 cup

¾ cups raw cashews

3 tbsp. nutritional yeast

¼ tsp. garlic powder

¾ tsp. sea salt

Add all ingredients to a food processor and pulse until a fine meal is achieved. Refrigerate until ready to use. Enjoy!

FLAX EGG REPLACEMENT

(as a binding ingredient, not as a breakfast meal!)

1 tbsp. flaxseed meal

2 ½ tbsp. water

Add flaxseed meal and water to a dish and whisk. Let rest for 5 minutes to thicken.

Use in desired recipe in place on 1 egg

COCONUT WHIPPED CREAM

Yields 2 cups

1 can coconut cream, chilled overnight

¾ cup powdered sugar

½ tsp. vanilla extract

Chill a large mixing bowl 10 minutes. Remove coconut cream can lid without tipping or shaking the can, keeping separation of the cream and liquid. Once opened, use a spoon to scrape the thickened cream and add to chilled mixing bowl. Discard remaining liquid or use for smoothies.

Beat chilled cream for 30 seconds with a mixer until cream. Add vanilla and powdered sugar and mix until creamy and smooth, about a minute. Use immediately or refrigerate, it will harden and set the longer it is chilled. Use to top your favorite dessert. Enjoy!

CPSIA information can be obtained
at www.ICGtesting.com
Printed in the USA
LVHW011931131120
671611LV00008B/336